At David C Cook, we equip the local church around
the corner and around the globe to make disciples.
Come see how we are working together—go to
www.davidccook.org. Thank you!

DAVID C COOK

transforming lives together

LETTERS TO THE CHURCH
STUDY GUIDE

LETTERS TO THE CHURCH
——— STUDY GUIDE ———

FRANCIS CHAN

DAVID **C** COOK

transforming lives together

LETTERS TO THE CHURCH STUDY GUIDE
Published by David C Cook
4050 Lee Vance Drive
Colorado Springs, CO 80918 U.S.A.

Integrity Music Limited, a Division of David C Cook
Eastbourne, East Sussex BN23 6NT, England

The graphic circle C logo is a registered trademark of David C Cook.

All epigraphs are excerpted from Francis Chan, *Letters to the
Church* (Colorado Springs: David C Cook, 2018).

ISBN 978-0-8307-7582-8
eISBN 978-0-8307-7627-6

The Team: Wendi Lord, Amy Konyndyk, Nick Lee,
Rachael Stevenson, Laura Derico, Susan Murdock
Cover Design: Jim Elliston

Special thanks to Laura Derico and the Crazy Love Team.

Printed in the United States of America
First Edition 2018

1 2 3 4 5 6 7 8 9 10

062818

CONTENTS

GETTING STARTED

God intends to change the world through the local church. The early church in the book of Acts was such a powerful force because the people were united in their pursuit of God's mission for the Church. They structured things around what they understood to be God's greatest desires for His Church. They were devoted to prayer, the apostles' teachings, one another, and Communion.

So many modern churches have strayed so far from this vision. This should break your heart. If we want to see revival in the Church, we are going to have to love her enough to press into these issues and not compromise when it gets hard. God wants to bring healing and renewal and a fresh outpouring of His Spirit on us. These are exciting times. God is moving, and there are a lot of people ready for reform.

Take a minute to dream about this. What if in our lifetime we could see the Church of God more excited about prayer, studying the Word, fellowship, and Communion than they are about a really good worship band, a well-crafted sermon, or great programs? What if we could see a Church where the majority are using their gifts to build up others rather than sitting passively for years only consuming? What if the great majority of the Church were thinking about how to use their time, resources, and lives for the furthering of the gospel rather than the furthering of their name or temporary lives here? If you are not yet committed to this dream, hopefully by the end of this process you will be. What better goal is there to give your life to?

This study is for electricians, nurses, teachers, kids, homeless people, cops, engineers, stay-at-home moms, church staff, tech people, and city workers. Being passionate about the Church has nothing to do with whether you work for a church. Nehemiah was cupbearer to the king (Neh. 1:11). He was more of a common worker, unlike Ezra, who was a scribe and priest (Ezra 7:11). Yet God burdened Nehemiah for the state of God's people and Jerusalem so much that he went back to rebuild the walls and God used him mightily. On top of that, in the New Testament we are all called a "royal priesthood" (1 Pet. 2:9). We are all workers in the church. God has called you to passionate, deep, full commitment to beautifying His body and Bride, regardless of age, gender, vocation, or anything else. Through this study you will be challenged to think and pray through what that would look like.

HOW TO GET THE MOST OUT OF THIS GUIDE

In these sessions, we will be breaking down some of the material discussed in the book *Letters to the Church*. To get the most out of this study, read through the corresponding chapter as you go through each session. Your experience can also be enhanced by using the material provided in the *Letters to the Church Video Series*. Each of these resources can stand alone, but they will be most effective together. Most importantly, it is essential for everyone to be reading this with a Bible on hand. Ultimately, the purpose of this study and the book is to point us back to the Bible and cause us to fall in love with God's original design for the Church.

USING THE STUDY GUIDE ON YOUR OWN

Whether you are doing this study with a group or as an individual, it is vital that you spend time going through the guide on your own. Your background and experiences are unique to you and will give you a perspective on this material no one else can offer. This book is meant to encourage you to reflect on your personal experience and push you to take these concepts beyond the theoretical and into practical application.

If you have *Letters to the Church*, reading the corresponding chapter straight through once before beginning the study guide session. Many of the questions and thoughts contained in the guide will refer to things from the reading, which you can reference and revisit as necessary. If you have the video series, you may find it helpful to watch the corresponding video at the beginning of your time, as this will set the vision of the chapter and give your mind a framework for the ideas you will be interacting with.

USING THE STUDY GUIDE IN A SMALL GROUP

If you are working through this material as part of a group, it is still important for you to go through the material on your own first (see the section above). This way the bulk of your time together can be spent in edifying one another through your discussion as opposed to getting familiar with content. Each person should come to the study with thoughts, questions, and reflections to add to the group discussion.

We recommend establishing a leader for the discussion group. This person doesn't need to have all the answers but should guide the conversation and move on to the next question when needed, in order to complete the session in the allotted time. At the same time, don't feel like you need to rush through things and bypass meaningful discussion in order to check the box of finishing the session. Be sensitive to the Spirit and open to which direction He would want to go. Maybe at points you need to stop and pray or worship for a while. Maybe God will do something totally different from what you are expecting. Be open.

It will also be helpful to create some ground rules for your time together. Depending on how this group came together, you may or may not have built trust, which is going to be huge for this study to be beneficial. It'd be sad if—as you're talking about the loving, powerful, unified Church—your group members were cutting off one another, not really hearing one another out, or not responding in love toward those who share something heavy on their hearts. Sometimes in a group it just takes one or two hurtful comments to cause people to be hesitant about being vulnerable. I would recommend going through these points as a group and agreeing to them together.

First, commit to using only words that build up one another.

Meditate on this passage as a group: "Let no corrupting talk come out of your mouths, but only such as is good for building up, as fits the occasion, that it may give grace to those who hear" (Eph. 4:29).

James also wrote about the power of our words and how it can be likened to a fire that can consume an entire forest (James 3:5). His exhortation to us is to tame our tongues so only words that bless come out of our mouths (v. 10). We are so careless with our words today. We're very quick to speak, when Scripture actually calls us to be slow to speak and quick to listen (1:19). Joking around and laughing with friends is often harmless and fun, but sometimes joking can go too far and hurt someone. Paul called us to such a high standard of making sure everything that comes out of our mouths builds up people and gives grace. If you can all agree to obeying this passage, your group will be much more effective.

Second, commit to not gossiping or slandering.

Gossip and slander are addressed in Scripture far more than we realize. They are often brought up in lists of other sins such as murder, hatred, greed, and arrogance (see, for example, Rom. 1:29–31; 2 Cor. 12:20). A big part of building trust is knowing that what we say won't be used against us. If you have a concern about what someone says, talk with that person directly rather than talking with others about it. God doesn't want us to talk about people in a way that causes others to think less of them. Can you imagine if you could look around at everyone in your group and know with 100 percent certainty that he or she would speak only well of you behind your back? This is the sort of community God desires. Commit to being that together and then hold one another to it if anyone says anything negative about someone else in the group.

Third, commit to getting everyone involved.

Some people tend to be really quiet, and some people tend to have a lot of thoughts and are comfortable expressing them. If you are quiet, try to speak up. Maybe you could make it a goal to share at least one thing each time you meet. You have something to contribute to the group that will bless others. If you tend to talk a lot, it's great you are contributing but be mindful of instances when you have spoken several times while others haven't spoken at all. Silence isn't a bad thing. Maybe those who are quiet need some silence to process what they are going to say.

Fourth, commit to letting the leader lead.

It's going to be really helpful to the flow of the sessions for everyone to allow the leader to guide the time. This will help prevent your group from getting off track or having extremely skewed levels of participation. Designate someone who can be the leader; otherwise you might end up spending your whole session discussing one question. Be mindful also of not bringing your own agenda into the discussion, steering the conversation into something else. Leaders should pay attention to the time and consider what pace to go at to try to complete the discussion.

NOTES FOR THE LEADER

When someone is leading well, everyone will reap the benefits but people won't be left thinking about the leader. You want to be strong in your leadership, but you also don't want to overlead. Examples of overleading would be talking more than anyone else, always feeling like you need to fill the time, not allowing others to take ownership of the discussion, or responding every time someone else talks instead of allowing free-flowing discussion to take place. Being a leader does not mean you have all the answers. Part of being a great leader is empowering people to answer one another's questions.

At the same time, you don't want to be passive by not addressing something unhealthy that is said, not moving the conversation forward when needed, or allowing Holy Spirit opportunities to pass when God is moving in someone and something needs to be addressed. You have a special opportunity to shape how this time is going to look. The pressure is by no means all on you to make the time meaningful, but by being sensitive to the leading of the Spirit, you can lead your group to press into what God is doing.

Be sensitive to the group and what is going on with them. If people are hurting and confessing something weighing heavy on them, it is more important to live out love tangibly than to keep doing the lesson on how we are supposed to love one another. Don't allow this study to be just about head knowledge. We can often make the mistake of thinking if content is downloaded into our brains, then it will change our lives. But it is likely that the most powerful part of this study isn't the content—it's the process of going through it together and the community that can come out of that. Maybe one of the best things you'll do as a leader is get people more involved in one another's lives in various ways.

Preparing for Each Session

Make sure you have read and processed through the chapter and study guide session before arriving at your group meeting. If you aren't familiar with the content, people will notice and will feel it's not important for them to read the material. You'll set the tone by your example. Also, spend some time praying for the people in the group. Again, this isn't primarily an intellectual exercise. It's spiritual. It's also relational, so be mindful to set a tone of love for one another. If this is a cold, formal group to you, it will probably be for them. If this is a time when deep relationships are forming for you, it will probably be for them.

Leading the Discussion

It will be helpful to look at the material before your group session and assess the speed needed to go through it in order to complete the discussion on time. Of course, if you don't finish it, that is fine, but considering the questions beforehand will help you generally know how long to take on each one. The questions build on one another, so it's helpful to go in order. If you aren't able to finish, encourage people to process the remaining questions on their own through the week and start the next week with a follow-up to that.

Fight the temptation to respond every time someone makes a comment. Instead, briefly affirm the comment and ask others to share to better cultivate dialogue.

Be okay with silence. People are thinking, and it's healthy for them to feel the weight of what to say. If after a while still no one has said anything, you could ask whether the question makes sense or possibly try to rephrase it for them.

Ultimately, the most important part of your leadership is not how you lead the discussion but how you lead your life. Do people see someone who loves Jesus intimately, who is submissive to whatever He says, who loves them deeply, and who is humble? If so, you are going to be an excellent leader. The success of your leadership before God is going to have much more to do with your character and love than your ability to speak eloquently.

1

THE DEPARTURE

*The strangest part about this season of my life
is that my intimacy with God has been directly
tied to my connection with the Church.*

VIDEO

Share session 1 from the *Letters to the Church Video Series* with your group. The video should be used at the beginning of your time together to introduce some of the concepts you will be discussing and to provide spiritual direction for the session.

DISCUSSION

The experience many Christians in the West have today in their churches looks very different from what we read in the New Testament. It is a scary thought that this has somehow become okay with us. God desires faith in His people, and it grieves His heart when we live in a way that shows we don't believe His promises and power are for us in the same way they were for the early church. The journey back to faithfulness won't be a quick one, and this book does not contain any magic formula to get us to where we are supposed to be. Change is going to require dedication and humility. We will have to lay down some things, like our desires and traditions, but it will be more than worth it. God has so much more for the Church to experience. Hopefully this vision will take root in your heart and push you to take action and pursue it.

1. Consider the thought exercise presented in the first few sentences of *Letters to the Church*. Write down

what you would understand church to be if the Bible was your only source of information. Compare that with your church experience. What are some discrepancies?

2. Reread the opening quotation to this session on page 19. Has this ever been true for you? Why or why not?

It is so important that this book not be viewed as a call to cause division. Over and over in the New Testament, the importance of unity within the Church is emphasized. We need to take an honest look at the state of the Church and be willing to consider and repent of the areas where we have fallen short. But we need to do it out of hearts of genuine love for the Church and respect for the authorities therein. It is easy to point fingers from the outside looking in, but that's not how change occurs. We need to come at this with an attitude of humility and not fall prey to the temptation to criticize or become defensive. It would be better for you to put down this book right now and stop reading than for it to become a tool for feeding pride and causing division. Nothing will destroy the Church faster than that kind of attitude.

We have all had hurts in the Church because it is filled with people who aren't perfect. But the challenge is to handle them well. Sometimes we can use those hurts as an excuse to speak against people or undermine people's confidence in leadership. We may think we are looking for support, but we are actually causing people to view others negatively. This is a big issue we must avoid. If you are hurt, it's important to go to the person who hurt you. If that person doesn't receive your words well, you can tell one other person in order to have them go with you. If they still don't receive what you are saying, then you include leadership at the church. This is what Jesus laid out in Matthew 18 as the process for dealing with sin. Behavior outside of this quickly becomes divisive.

3. Have you ever found yourself unintentionally speaking against another believer, causing others to view him or her negatively? What caused you to do that?

Without using names and doing further damage, spend some time repenting and deciding to stop doing this going forward.

4. In 1 Samuel 24 and 26, David had opportunities to remove King Saul from power and claim the throne he had been promised by God. But he didn't do it. Read 1 Samuel 24:6 for David's response. This attitude of deference toward one God placed in a position of authority seems foreign in today's context. Have you ever been guilty of displaying a critical attitude toward people in leadership in the Church? List some of the reasons for behaving that way. Beside each reason, write one way you could have handled the situation differently instead of responding with criticism. Share some examples with one another.

There are times when God hates our worship. That statement was probably hard for many of you to read. It was not written lightly. It is a difficult reality to accept. But we all need to be willing to consider the possibility that our worship is displeasing. Worship is not about our feelings; it is all about God. He is the object of our worship, and His thoughts should be our sole concern when we come together to worship. So often we are busy thinking about what we or others want while neglecting what God wants in His Church! And it's not as though we have to go around guessing about what God wants. God gave us Scripture to guide us in our pursuit of Him, and we need to start heeding what it says, even when it is difficult to accept.

5. Read through Malachi 1:6–14. Notice that the people did not see anything wrong with their offering. Why do you think that is? What about their attitude or their worship was displeasing to God?

6. How we behave—how much we give of ourselves— reflects how we view God. If we just show up to services, serve in a ministry or two, and give money to our church but do little else for the Church the rest of the week, what does that really say about how we view God? Should we assume God is pleased? He demands everything and is pleased with nothing less. What weaknesses can you identify in your commitment to the Church? How can you address them?

The reality is that many people try to change what it means to worship God because they don't want to do what He has asked. When you look at your heart and life, do you see someone who is willing to do whatever God asks? Or do you see someone who will be in a church as long as God doesn't ask too much of you? We can come up with so many arguments to defend our way of life or decisions we make in our churches, but what is most important is that we are willing to do whatever He wants.

7. As you've begun reading *Letters to the Church* and this study guide, do you sense yourself getting defensive or protective of what you're used to with the church? Anytime you sense yourself getting defensive or coming up with a counterargument, think of that as a red flag—a time to stop and consider, *Why am I feeling this way? Am I being open to whatever God wants?* Share with your group any statements in this study so far that have made you feel uncomfortable, guilty, or defensive. Be open to learning about what those reactions tell you about yourself and your relationship with God.

These are serious and weighty topics. It is easy to get overwhelmed in the face of what seems like a very daunting task. But we can take comfort in the fact that, ultimately, God has a vision for the Church and He will empower us for the work required to achieve that vision. We need to take ownership of and be devoted to stewarding the Church well, but we can also find rest in knowing that we are simply joining in what He is already doing.

8. Read Revelation 3:19–21. Rejoice at the fact that Jesus stood knocking at the door of a church that had a lot of issues. If Jesus came knocking on your church's door, what would be some of the responses people would have?

9. Write down or share with one another some moments in your life or experiences you've had when you have seen God do amazing things. Think of times you have had your prayers answered. Think of stories in the Bible that display God's faithfulness. Let these things fill you with confidence and hope for what He will do in your church.

We need to live in light of the eternity that is coming very soon. As we have been discussing, this means we need to live with hope and vision for what the Church here on earth can be. But it also means living with a sense of urgency. We need to be willing to lay aside anything that hinders us or any sin that could entangle us in our pursuit (Heb. 12:1). This is so much more important.

10. Take some time to pray together. Ask God to give each of you a passion for His Church and a dedication to her health. Pray for a heart of humility and grace as you examine yourself and your church. Pray that God would direct your steps and give you a spirit of boldness and urgency as you pursue this mission.

2

SACRED

We have cheapened something sacred, and we must repent.

VIDEO

Share session 2 from the *Letters to the Church Video Series* with your group. The video should be used at the beginning of your time together to introduce some of the concepts you will be discussing and to provide spiritual direction for the session.

DISCUSSION

Job had a lot of thoughts about God. From his perspective, even as a righteous man, he felt God owed him an explanation and was even potentially wrong in what He had done. For almost the entirety of the book of Job, he and a few other men are going back and forth, talking about their opinions of how God operates. After all this, God finally spoke to Job, and here is Job's response in Job 40:4–5: "I am of small account; what shall I answer you? I lay my hand on my mouth. I have spoken once, and I will not answer; twice, but I will proceed no further."

God continued to rebuke Job for his arrogance, and then Job responded again in Job 42:2–6: "I know that you can do all things, and that no purpose of yours can be thwarted. 'Who is this that hides counsel without knowledge?' Therefore I have uttered what I did not understand, things too wonderful for me, which I did not know. 'Hear, and I will speak; I will question you, and you make it known to me.' I had heard of you by the hearing of the ear, but now my eye sees you; therefore I despise myself, and repent in dust and ashes."

There was something Job didn't understand until he encountered God. God is sacred. You don't play around with Him. He's not your buddy. He's not common. He's not someone to be taken lightly. Job never made that mistake again. The challenge for us is that we are so used to common things and we quickly forget God is different. Somehow we have to fight this tendency and remember what God said in Isaiah: "For my thoughts are not your thoughts, neither are your ways my ways, declares the LORD. For as the heavens are higher than the earth, so are my ways higher than your ways and my thoughts than your thoughts" (55:8–9).

Our culture teaches us to push back on everything. We are so quick to question authority and to assume we are in the right. That attitude is oftentimes misplaced, even when directed toward imperfect human authorities. But it is completely inappropriate when we bring it into our relationship with God.

1. As a group, read through at least two of the situations mentioned at the beginning of chapter 2 of *Letters to the Church*: Uzzah touching the ark (2 Sam. 6), King Saul's sacrifice (1 Sam. 13), Moses striking the rock (Num. 20), Ananias and Sapphira lying about their donation (Acts 5), and the Corinthians celebrating

Communion in an unworthy manner (1 Cor. 11). Then consider, What is striking about the situations to you? Why? What do these situations show you about God?

2. Take a minute to define *sacred*. Would you say that in your church experience, God is treated as sacred? Why or why not?

When we truly understand the sacredness of God, we can't help but marvel at the mystery of the Church. The idea that we can commune intimately with the Creator of the universe and He *desires* us to should cause us to fall on our faces in awe. Yet we have come to treat it as common. We feel a constant need to move on to the next thing, the newest thing, the better thing. We need to kill that culture within the Church. It doesn't get any better than this. If you find yourself underwhelmed or wishing for more, you need to reevaluate your understanding of these realities. We need to rediscover the beauty of the simple truths of the gospel and allow them to permeate every part of our lives.

3. Read Ephesians 5:29–32 as many times as it takes for it to really sink in. When was the last time you were amazed by this truth?

The Church is a living temple of God. This has vast implications for all of us individually but also collectively. No one block can be the temple by itself, but at the same time each block is essential for the temple to function most effectively. We need to value one another and encourage one another faithfully.

4. Read 2 Chronicles 7:1–4; Acts 2:1–4, 37–47; 1 Corinthians 3:16–17; and Ephesians 2:19–22; 3:8–10. Compare the idea of the temple in the Old Testament being the dwelling place of God with God's people presented as the temple in the New Testament. What are the implications of that?

5. What behaviors or attitudes of our own might change if we were to treat our brothers and sisters in Christ as blocks in a holy temple that transcends time and space?

6. Think about how we so often critique things we do or don't like about the church and the leadership of

it. How is this a problem in light of God and His
Church being sacred?

What is a tremendous, unspeakable honor may feel
insufficient for those who are used to being god of their own
blogs and Twitter accounts. So often when we look forward
to heaven, it is the rewards—the lack of sickness, sorrow, and
suffering—that we dwell on. But in doing so, we're missing
the whole point. Heaven is the restoration of God's original
intent for humanity. We will once again dwell with Him and
experience the fullness of His presence. That is our hope. God
wants us to long for that with all our hearts. It is *all* about
Him. Society conditions us to be self-centered, but there is
no room for this in the Church. God's glory is too sacred; we
can't afford to compromise on this. We need to take our eyes
off ourselves and regain a heavenly perspective.

Think about going to see a highly anticipated movie or
the Super Bowl. Are you disappointed there are a lot of people
there? No, you are probably actually excited to see so many
people who enjoy the event as much as you do. There is a

camaraderie with everyone there. You're not the focus, but you love it still. This is a small taste of what heaven will be like—where we are part of a large crowd of people yet are so excited because we all adore our King together. We lose self-focus yet gain so much more. The more we look at ourselves, the more we will get depressed. The more we look at Christ, the more joy fills our hearts.

7. Are you excited for heaven? What about heaven most excites you?

8. How have you seen self-centeredness manifest itself in your life? In your church? What are some practical ways you can help yourself and others bring the focus back to what really matters?

For most of this session we have focused on how we need to have a greater reverence for God. At this point, it is important for us to remember that God Himself designed the Church. He calls her His Bride. He made her intentionally, and she is beautiful to Him. We have a responsibility to be faithful to that design, and many of us have strayed far from it. Out of reverence and love for God, we need to love His Church enough to dedicate ourselves to her.

9. Meditate on Ephesians 3:8–10 together. What do you think it means? Do you think the "manifold wisdom of God" can be seen through your church? Why or why not?

10. Do you truly love the Church? Or some weeks is attending church just a box to check?

11. Spend some time in prayer on your own and with your group. Be honest with the Lord about the condition of your heart toward Him and His Church. Repent of the times when you have cheapened the sacred things of God. Ask Him to show you the areas in your life and in your ministry where you have strayed from His design, and then pray for the strength to change.

3

THE ORDER

*It is imperative that we differentiate between
what we want and what God commands.*

VIDEO

Share session 3 from the *Letters to the Church Video Series* with your group. The video should be used at the beginning of your time together to introduce some of the concepts you will be discussing and to provide spiritual direction for the session.

DISCUSSION

Are we giving God what He asked for? This is a really important question! In Luke 12 and Matthew 25, Jesus told parables to stress the importance of us being serious about God's commands. He clearly taught that there is a day coming when God will hold us accountable for whether or not we did as He told us. On that day it won't suffice to say, "Well, at least I gave You something, right?" He isn't looking for just *something*. He is looking for obedience to what He asked for. Remember the example of going to a restaurant and ordering a steak only to receive a plate of spaghetti. You aren't thinking in that moment, *Well, at least he gave me something.*

Read Mark 7:1–13 together.

1. Notice that the Pharisees were forcing people to wash their hands before they ate. But God never told people they needed to do this. Make some observations about Jesus' response to the Pharisees. Why

was He so upset? What words did He repeat? What seems to be the focus in His strong rebuke of the Pharisees?

2. It's obvious that washing your hands before you eat isn't a bad thing. It's actually a good idea. The problem was that it became a higher priority to people than what God actually asked for. Complete one of the exercises mentioned in the book. Below you will find space to make two lists. In the "Commands (Not Optional)" section, start listing out scriptural commanded God has given us as new covenant believers. Be sure that these are actual commands, not merely things we see happen in the Bible or feel are good ideas. Then in the "Traditions (Optional)" column, write out things that tend to be frequently expected in churches today but aren't actually commanded. An example of this could be "dressing up," since there is nothing in Scripture that commands us to do it but often it is expected in the church. Think through

concepts such as "having a really good church service," "sermons," "youth group," and "nice meeting places." If something isn't commanded, it doesn't mean it's a bad thing; it just means it is optional. The goal is not to figure out every single difficult issue and debate it for an extended period of time, but rather to come up with two lists relatively quickly. Hopefully you can do most of this during personal time but if not, take five minutes to write and then spend some time as a group sharing your answers.

Commands (Not Optional)	Traditions (Optional)

3. Now that you have your two lists, discuss what you tend to give more time, money, and energy toward personally and as a church. Do we get more upset if we aren't taking things on the command side seriously or if we aren't taking things on the tradition side seriously?

Read 1 Corinthians 1:13–17 and 2:1–5 together. We know from 2 Corinthians 10–11 that this church wanted an eloquent preacher (or superapostle) to look up to and elevate. But Paul refused to let them make it about him. He chose not to baptize many of them or to preach with eloquence so their "faith might not rest in the wisdom of men but in the power of God" (1 Cor. 2:5). He wanted to depend on the power of the gospel rather than his own effort, "lest the cross of Christ be emptied of its power" (1:17). Jesus was also very careful to not let people make following Him become about something else. In John 6, He fed a large crowd of people, who then followed Him around hoping for more food. Jesus refused even though He could have kept them around, by giving them what they wanted. He was left with the people who really wanted Him and Him alone.

4. Are we content in the Church today with seeing people who don't really love Jesus walk away from the Church? Or do we try to keep them? Explain.

5. If a certain decision in the Church will help us get more people to come, does that mean it is definitely something we should do? Why or why not? At what point would it become a bad thing?

6. Imagine you saw Muslims from a local mosque using raffles, putting on big concerts, investing in fancy facilities, and using other gimmicks to draw people in to join their religion. What would you think about that? What would it say about the appeal of their

god? What would you assume about the motivations of the followers of that religion? Now imagine that mosque again, but change it to a Christian church. Have we ever been guilty of using a show to draw people to God instead of letting God show Himself to people? How?

7. In India, people will walk for miles just to come and pray with the church because they love prayer and fellowship and Jesus. What do you think it says about a church if people won't come just for prayer, reading Scripture together, and loving one another? What does it say about us if we need really good bands, lively preachers, great programs, and elaborate facilities to be motivated to attend a church?

8. How should we respond if we do need all these other things?

Read Acts 2:42–47 together. The early church "devoted themselves to the apostles' teaching and the fellowship, to the breaking of bread and the prayers" (v. 42). *Devoted* is a really important word in that sentence. Sometimes we have been guilty of being devoted to sermons or Christian books more than to the apostles' teaching. There is nothing that can replace reading the Word of God. Hebrews 4:12 says, "The word of God is living and active." When we read Scripture, it acts on us in a way no other words can. Sometimes we have also been guilty of being more devoted to programs than to one another. We may be faithful to attend things, but few people in our church would call us "faithful" to them personally. There was also something about the early church's commitment to the Lord's Supper and prayer that we often fall short of.

9. As a group, define the word *devoted*. It's important to think about this word as we evaluate our hearts to see whether it is true of us.

10. When you look at yourself and your church, would you say you are devoted to the apostles' teaching? To the breaking of bread? To fellowship? To prayer?

11. Spend some time in prayer responding to God with what you have discovered about yourself and where you may be falling short in taking His commands seriously. Ask Him what He wants you to do about what you've discovered.

4

THE GANG

*What if we took God's description of the
Church as a family seriously?*

VIDEO

Share session 4 from the *Letters to the Church Video Series* with your group. The video should be used at the beginning of your time together to introduce some of the concepts you will be discussing and to provide spiritual direction for the session.

DISCUSSION

Think about a group of people extremely unified and committed to one another. What groups come to mind? Isn't it sad that most people wouldn't think about the Church? A family would probably be first. Then our minds might go to gangs or even possibly sports teams, fraternities, or clubs before we think of the Church. But Jesus is creating a new community where the commitment is far greater than anywhere else.

1. Jesus felt more committed and connected to believers than to His biological family. Read Matthew 12:46–50 together. Have you ever experienced the Church as a closer family for you than your own biological family? If you have, what was that like? Tell about that experience.

2. Read John 13:34–35 out loud. What is supposed to set us apart as disciples of Jesus Christ? Can you name any church that is famous for the way its members love one another? Name some of the things that churches are often known for instead.

One of the primary markers of a church's health in Paul's mind was how well they loved one another. Check out 2 Thessalonians 1:3: "We ought always to give thanks to God for you, brothers, as is right, because your faith is growing abundantly, and the love of every one of you for one another is increasing." Think about the two reasons Paul gave for his thankfulness: first, their faith was growing (which was an obvious big deal); and second, their love for one another was increasing. Check out Ephesians 1:15–16, where Paul said something similar to the Ephesian church: "For this reason, because I have heard of your faith in the Lord Jesus and your love toward all the saints, I do not cease to give thanks for you, remembering you in my prayers." Paul was so thankful because he heard about their faith in Jesus (again, obviously a huge deal) and their love toward all the saints.

3. Faith and love for one another aren't the only markers of a healthy church, but they are two really important ones in the Bible. What other qualities have we often thought of as important markers of a healthy church? Evaluate them against what is said to be important in Scripture.

4. If our love for one another is one of the primary determiners of the health of our churches, take a moment to assess your church based just on that. Does your love for one another continuously increase? Would Paul be rejoicing as he heard people talk about your church? Explain your answers.

In the last session, we looked at commands versus traditions and how we have to prioritize commands. A command from God is sacred and important, even if He says it only one time. How do you think we should treat a command if God was to say it over fifty times? As a child, when your mom told you to clean your room, you probably knew it was something you should do. But if she was to tell you fifty times to do it, hopefully you would understand that it is extremely important to her. And if we respect our moms enough to obey them, how much more should we respect God enough to obey whatever He asks of us?

We are commanded to love one another over fifty times in the New Testament. It is one of the strongest emphases in the entire New Testament. To get a feel for just how much God emphasizes loving one another, take time as a group to read through a list of "one another" commands (which isn't even totally comprehensive) in the back of this book. Go around the group and have each person read a couple from the list.

We don't take these commands as seriously as we need to. "Do not murder," "do not steal," "do not bear false witness," and other commands like these tend to feel really important. If someone was to steal, we wouldn't hesitate to call that a sin. But if people don't make their love increase and overflow for the believers in their church body, do any of us think of it as sin? Or what if someone doesn't care to encourage other believers? That's a command repeated four times in Scripture

(1 Thess. 4:18; 5:11, 14; 2 Thess. 3:12)! What if someone isn't willing to be open and vulnerable and therefore disobeys the command to "love one another earnestly, from a pure heart" (1 Pet. 1:22)? Would we think of that person as being sinful?

5. Take a couple of minutes to discuss whether your experience has been that we take these commands seriously in our churches. You may have confronted someone about being rude, but have you ever confronted someone for not loving deeply enough? Do you think people in your church would confront the issue of not being in deep relationship with one another?

6. If you feel that we aren't taking these commands seriously enough, discuss how you think we arrived at that point. What has influenced our view of the importance of loving one another? What reasons do people—even Christians—use sometimes to excuse the fact that they aren't showing love to one another

as much as they should? It's important to understand this so we can do something about it.

7. What would it look like if love was the main quality that stood out in our church gatherings? Take time to picture that. Think about what might currently be making it more difficult to love one another. Write down some ideas and share them with the group.

Sometimes our problem is that we are so busy doing other stuff in the Church that we don't have time for relationships. One thing we might need to repent of is being too busy with seemingly good things that are keeping us from more important things. Most of us don't develop deep relationships primarily through scheduled meetings. They are almost always built through life together: living together, working together, going to school together, or some other way where our lives overlap a lot. Maybe it won't work for us to just try harder to fit relationships into our overly scheduled lives. Maybe we are going to have to do some massive overhaul. So many of us are way too busy. And even with our programmed activities, we need to be more intentional. If you're going to watch the game, why not invite people from the church to watch with you? You eat dinner every night. Why not have more people over to eat together, in community? Maybe you have an extra bedroom. Why not offer that room to someone in the church so you can do life together?

Take a moment to read Acts 2:42–47 and 4:32–35.

8. As a group, go through these passages line by line and list qualities or actions characteristic of the Church as described in these verses. Which of these are reflected in your own church? Which are not?

9. Do you believe it would be possible for the Church to look like this today? What has led you to have hope about this? What has discouraged you from believing this?

Our culture affects the way we view the Bible and Christianity. If you're in the US, you've probably been heavily influenced by individualism and idolize productivity in ways you don't even realize. Scripture paints a different picture of Christianity, saying everyone in the early church shared everything. Not just some people, but rather, "no one said that any of the things that belonged to him was his own, but they had everything in common" (Acts 4:32). They were all on board with this. You need a car? Here's mine. You need somewhere to live? Move on in. You need money? Let me empty out my bank account. Seem crazy? This is Christianity. But how in the world could the Church back then love one another that much? For starters, they weren't just meeting on Sunday for ninety minutes. They were meeting "day by day" (2:46) and seemed to really love having meals together in homes. It wasn't about formal meetings. They were family. They loved being around one another and were doing so constantly. Yet we are often so sheltered from one another and isolated. Something has to change. We can't keep disobeying God.

10. What sort of changes do you think are needed within your life to create space for deeper relationships? Don't hide behind generalities like "I should stop watching TV as much" or "I want to try to have people over more." Figure out some tangible things to hold one another accountable to do. Do you need to sell your home? Move someone into your home? Change your job? They don't have to be really big things, but if you are seeing that there is a big gap between your life and Scripture, don't rule out big changes.

11. Now ask yourself this: Are you really going to make these changes? It's so easy to fall back into your normal routine. It's going to take focus and accountability to make changes. Revisit this. How are you going to make sure you don't just forget about this?

Loving one another deeply from the heart, encouraging one another, being devoted to one another, and so many other things we read earlier are not optional. We're going to stand before Jesus soon, and He really expects us to be loving one another radically compared with the world. We have to make whatever changes are necessary. Don't do it six months from now. Make the changes now.

5

SERVANTS

Only when we become servants will we experience the Holy Spirit as Jesus intended. Only then will the Church resemble the Christ they worship.

VIDEO

Share session 5 from the *Letters to the Church Video Series* with your group. The video should be used at the beginning of your time together to introduce some of the concepts you will be discussing and to provide spiritual direction for the session.

DISCUSSION

How often do you gather with your church, thinking about how you could best serve the body? Sadly this has become a very foreign attitude within the Church. We have designed church services so the majority of the congregation does not have to do anything. The kids are taken care of, someone leads a time of worship for everyone, and someone else breaks down the Word. Everything is geared toward the convenience and comfort of the congregation. It is a shockingly consumerist arrangement no one seems to even question.

There is a huge flaw in this system! God did not intend for His Church to be a body of consumers. His Word says He uniquely gifted each person with something to contribute (1 Cor. 12). If only a few people are exercising their gifts, the body will be weaker for it. Can you imagine if you had two healthy legs but only ever used one of them? Sure, you could make some kind of crutch or hop to get around, but you would be nowhere near your full potential. It would be ridiculous to settle for that limited range of motion when you have the ability to run. But that's what we're doing in the Church when we have only a couple of people using their gifts; we're handicapping ourselves, and we're never going to reach our full potential.

1. How many people are in your church? About how many of those people are contributing (not just financially) in a meaningful way to the life of the body so others are being blessed by them? Do the math and write down the percentage. If that number is less than 100 percent, are you content to settle for that?

2. What are some strengths or giftings the Lord has given you? How do you use those in the context of the Church? How could you exercise them more?

Read through Philippians 2:1–9 slowly, verse by verse.

3. Consider the mind-set of Jesus, which Paul told us to have among ourselves. Jesus exemplified radical humility and servanthood. Jesus modeled laying down His rights and comforts for the sake of others. When do you tend to focus not on the interests of others but rather on your own?

4. Paul wrote that believers should have "the same love, being in full accord and of one mind" (v. 2). What do you think it would look like for a group of believers to live unified in the mind-set of laying down their rights for the sake of their brothers and sisters in Jesus? How would it look the same or different from your current experience?

We tend to view serving and considering others more important as a burden or a task that has to be done rather than a joy. In reality, focusing only on yourself is the most miserable way to live. Being a servant is not a box you need to check once a week in order to be a good Christian; servanthood is supposed to be our identity as Christ-followers. It is a lifestyle, and the people who live it are often the most joyful people in the room.

5. Imagine you are attending your church for the first time as a nonbeliever. You've heard that Christians are supposed to love one another the way Christ does, sacrificing to the point of death. As you spend time with the members of your church, would the way the church serves one another stand out to you as supernatural and like Jesus?

6. Now think of the most servant-hearted person you know. Imagine if every person in your church loved

serving like that. How would that change the experience of a first-time attender?

Because today's culture is so self-focused, we don't take selfishness as seriously as we ought. Just as servanthood is beautiful to God, selfishness is ugly to Him. It is a sin we need to be willing to confront in ourselves and an issue we need to be willing to call out in others in a loving way. Becoming a Christian is taking on the name of Christ, who is the ultimate servant. We can't feed into a culture of selfishness in the Church; we risk cultivating a group of "Christians" who think it is okay not to be Christlike.

Sometimes we make excuses for why we don't serve by saying we don't have the ability to fill certain roles or others could do it better. This kind of self-deprecation is very unbiblical. The Bible tells us each believer is given a gift from the Holy Spirit for the common good of the body. We are meant to walk in humility, knowing that any gifts we have are from God, but we are also meant to walk in confidence and power, knowing that God desires to use us.

7. Read 1 Corinthians 12:7 and 14:12. Do you believe the Holy Spirit is in you? Do you believe God created you with gifts to bless His people? If not, stop and meditate on these Scriptures and ask God to give you the faith to believe His words. If you do believe in these gifts, spend some time considering whether your life is lining up with your beliefs.

Sometimes there are people who have gifts and are ready to use them, but there just isn't space for it. Most gatherings have little room for deviation in the agenda. Many small groups don't have leadership within the church to guide the use of gifts. Then we expect people to figure out how to use their gifts on their own. Of course, we should be using the spiritual gifts in all of life, but we need a context to help train people and for leaders to be present in that context. So in what church context do we expect to see the exercising of spiritual gifts by everyone in the body? Part of the issue is that we are often uncomfortable with silence and feel as though we need a plan to execute. But how do you plan the spontaneous use of gifts we see in Scripture?

8. Read 1 Corinthians 14:26–40. What do you notice about their gatherings here? How many people seem to have been contributing? Did it seem as though they made a plan ahead of time? There is a call to peace (v. 33) and order (v. 40), but that is in the midst of various people spontaneously being inspired to contribute to the gathering. Do you see these types of gatherings happening in your church?

9. In what context do you think you can see people being expected to exercise their gifts in the body? How do you help train and activate people?

We would never dream of looking God in the face and telling Him we thought one of His children was worthless. But we don't have to say it with our lips if our actions scream it. In the flesh, we are all very judgmental people. We can put too much emphasis on certain kinds of people—gifted speakers, worship leaders, etc.—and overlook others. This is dangerous in the Church. The Bible tells us that each individual is vital to the healthy functioning of the Church. Just as we have a responsibility to use the giftings we have been given to serve the body, we have a responsibility to empower other people to operate within their giftings and to treat each person as an invaluable member of the body.

10. Do you consciously focus on empowering others to see them activated? If not, who are some people you could be intentional with in this way? Write down their names and pray for them. If you feel led, reach out to them with a word of encouragement.

11. Take some time to pray. Ask God to help you walk with a balance of humility and confidence. Ask Him for confidence in His desire to move powerfully through you. Ask Him for the strength to step out in faith and start exercising your gifts, even when it is uncomfortable. Ask Him to use you to encourage and empower other believers to do the same. Then trust Him to move.

6

GOOD SHEPHERDS

*May God continue to raise up an army of good shepherds
who love Him above all else and live to make the
Church become everything God designed it to be.*

VIDEO

Share session 6 from the *Letters to the Church Video Series* with your group. The video should be used at the beginning of your time together to introduce some of the concepts you will be discussing and to provide spiritual direction for the session.

DISCUSSION

Saul was going to become the first king of Israel. When people first saw him, it made sense to them that he would be king because he looked the part: tall and handsome. We are introduced to him when his father sent him with a servant to find some donkeys (1 Sam. 9). He proved himself incompetent in fulfilling this seemingly simple task and then was ready to quit and go home. Though Saul was supposed to be the leader, his servant is the one who came up with the good idea to go see the prophet Samuel. Adding to these two failures, Saul wasn't prepared to give Samuel a gift to honor him. But the servant was. Who seems to be the more qualified leader in this scenario? Clearly the servant. Yet when they met Samuel, he anointed Saul as the new king.

David was going to become the second king of Israel. When people first saw *him*, it didn't make any sense to them why he should be king. He didn't look the part. In fact, when Samuel the prophet came to David's home looking for the next king, nobody seemed to think David should be there. Even Samuel looked at one of David's older brothers and assumed God would choose him to be king, based on appearances. God had to teach Samuel: "Do not look on his appearance or on the height of his stature, because I have rejected him. For the LORD sees not as man sees: man looks on the outward appearance, but the LORD looks on the heart" (1 Sam. 16:7). So where was this next king of Israel while all his brothers were gathered to their father with the prophet? He was "keeping the sheep" (v. 11).

Several verses later, when Saul was calling for David to play music for him, he said, "Send me David your son, who is with the sheep" (v. 19). David was so faithful to care for his father's sheep that it was what he was known for.

Later when the Philistines were terrorizing the army of Israel and three of David's brothers were there serving Saul, David was still going back and forth from the battle to ensure the sheep were cared for. You would think he might drop his responsibility with the sheep in order to focus on the Philistines, but he didn't. He cared for the sheep. He was a good shepherd. He was faithful with what he had been entrusted with, regardless of how small it might have seemed. David went to the battle only because his father told him to do so, and even then he ensured the flock was cared for in his absence by placing a shepherd over them

(17:12–20). When he learned of Goliath's defiance of God's army, it was David's faithfulness in caring for his father's sheep that served as his résumé.

It is here that we learn the most amazing aspect of David's care for his father's flock: he had risked his life multiple times to fight off bears and lions to protect the sheep. Now if David cared deeply enough about mere animals that he was willing to risk his life for them, do you think he was going to do a good job caring for God's people?

The author of 1 Samuel intended to teach us something through the contrast of Saul and David. It's a lesson that isn't very different from one Jesus taught: "One who is faithful in a very little is also faithful in much, and one who is dishonest in a very little is also dishonest in much" (Luke 16:10). One of the best determinants for whether people will be good leaders is how faithful they are before God with the little things. Do they have gentleness and patience with their family members? Do they live a simple life, rejecting greed and using their money generously? Are they hospitable, willing to bring people into their homes? Do they give time to relationships, prioritizing discipleship and caring deeply for people? Are they humble, rejecting the temptation to ambitious self-promotion? The world looks at gifting, eloquence, experience, and ability. God looks at character and the heart.

1. Read 1 Timothy 3:1–7 and Titus 1:5–9. What do you notice about the requirements for the highest level of leadership in the local church? Do those requirements seem to be about character or ability?

2. Do you think we typically view leadership as being about godly character rather than ability? If not, why do you think that is?

3. Why do we tend to elevate those like Saul (people who have the outward signs of a leader—such as charisma, eloquence, gifting) rather than those like David (people who have humility and godly character)?

Take a minute to recall the characteristics of a pastor in chapter 6 of *Letters to the Church*: Christian, praying, humble, loving, equipping, Spirit-filled, missional, and suffering.

4. Which of these characteristics do you think are usually valued strongly in a normal church?

5. Which of these characteristics do you think are most often neglected in a typical view of church leadership? Why do you think that is?

Though these characteristics should be in all formal leaders in the church, they should also be in every single Christian. Hopefully you weren't spending all your time evaluating your leaders but were also evaluating yourself. We mentioned earlier how David was a great leader and Saul was a terrible one. But while Saul was in charge, David refused to dishonor him or attack him (1 Sam. 24, 26); he had such respect for God's authority. Likewise, we need to be really careful to not become arrogant and use this book in a way that undermines and dishonors those God has put above us. We are called to be under human spiritual authority, and that authority will always be flawed.

6. Think about this command: "Obey your leaders and submit to them, for they are keeping watch over your souls, as those who will have to give an account.

Let them do this with joy and not with groaning, for that would be of no advantage to you" (Heb. 13:17). How can we guard against using this material in a way that disobeys this passage? Brainstorm with your group ways you can bring your leaders more joy and less groaning.

7. Think specifically about the humble pastor. We live in very arrogant times, when people think their opinions matter a lot. When do you see yourself sharing your opinion more than God's truth? How do you cultivate humility in your life?

8. For you personally, which characteristic was most convicting to read about?

9. Why do you think you've struggled with that? How do you want to address it?

All our pastors and elders in the San Francisco Bay Area have jobs outside the church. Many of them don't have any formal education for ministry. Many of them are not eloquent. They wouldn't necessarily be looked to for leadership. But they love Jesus, love people, and love the Word of God. For us that's the requirement. This is not to say pastors can't have their employment from the church. But we need to change what we have set as the bar for pastors. Thinking someone will be a good pastor because he or she is a gifted speaker, is a strong administrator, and has a lot of experience is like picking someone to be on your basketball team because that person can bench-press five hundred pounds. It's not a holistic measurement.

Some of you reading this may have assumed you aren't supposed to be a leader in the church because you don't have a certain level of gifting or formal training. But if godliness is what qualifies someone, then you have no excuse. This is not about titles or roles necessarily but rather about taking responsibility for caring for others spiritually. Every one of you reading this can become someone who leads others whether you are a stay-at-home mom, a full-time teacher, working in tech, a cop, a construction worker, or a financial consultant (we have significant leaders in our church in each of these vocations).

10. If the requirement for being a leader in the church is godly character, think about what that means for you. In what ways might God be wanting you to take on more responsibility for others in their spiritual formation? Have you ever had a thought that someone should _____ in the church (fill in the blank with a task or responsibility you felt was not being covered in your church)? What made you think that "someone" wasn't you?

If you don't feel as if you are able to care for others spiritually, that means you must feel you have serious sin in your life, since the qualifier for leadership is godliness. Did you ever realize your sin is hurting others? There are a lot of people around you both inside and outside the church who need you to show them Jesus, invest in them, carry burdens with them, and teach them things. But if your character is preventing you from doing that, they are suffering for it.

To close out this session, spend some time confessing sin. It would be so tempting to end the session right now before doing this. Don't. The next few minutes could be a turning point for you. Are there things you've done recently you know aren't right but you're hiding them? One of the most freeing things that can happen in your life is to bring these things to light. Be honest about yourself. Jesus said, "Nothing is covered up that will not be revealed, or hidden that will not be known. Therefore whatever you have said in the dark shall be heard in the light, and what you have whispered in private rooms shall be proclaimed on the housetops" (Luke 12:2–3). Do you see what Jesus was saying? Everything we've done in secret is going to be revealed soon.

Look around the room right now at the people you're with. Imagine if all your thoughts and actions over the last couple of months were put on a screen for them to watch. *Everything.* Would that freak you out? This is exactly what is going to happen after this life. All will be exposed. Why not do it now while you can still deal with it and change? Better now than at the judgment seat. It is an amazing feeling to live without the shame and hiding that come from unconfessed sin.

Split into smaller groups of two or three—men with men, women with women—to confess sin. Don't let Satan keep you quiet anymore. If this is a group in which you don't know one another well, make plans right now in your groups, at minimum, to have a conversation with someone in your church this week to confess your sin and turn from it. It's time to be the shepherd you've been called to be.

7

CRUCIFIED

*According to Jesus, far from having no cost, following
Him will cost you everything. Far from promising
a better life, He warned of intense suffering.*

VIDEO

Share session 7 from the *Letters to the Church Video Series* with your group. The video should be used at the beginning of your time together to introduce some of the concepts you will be discussing and to provide spiritual direction for the session.

DISCUSSION

Jesus did not give altar calls—at least not the way we understand them. He didn't spend His time trying to persuade anyone that He was worthy of being followed. They either got it or they didn't. In fact, oftentimes in the New Testament you find Jesus cautioning people against committing to follow Him if they were not ready to make the necessary sacrifices (see, for example, Matt. 16:24). He wasn't interested in drawing thousands of people for a surface-level faith. Jesus devoted Himself to raising up a few disciples who understood the cost and knew beyond a shadow of a doubt that He was worth everything.

In today's churches, we no longer teach that this kind of faith is necessary. We have created a culture where people can call themselves Christians as long as they go to services on Sunday and then they can live however they want for the rest of the week. As a result, we have cultivated an attitude of apathy and detachment. We have watered down the gospel to the point where it no longer requires any commitment or faith.

If a father tells his son to take out the trash every day but then the father proceeds to do it himself each time, he's not really teaching his son to do his chores, is he? He's actually teaching him that he doesn't need to, regardless of what he says to his face. We can preach the cost of discipleship from the pulpit, but if we don't *expect* the cost of discipleship in the lives of the people around us, we are still in error and allowing for a watered down gospel. If we allow people to attend the church for two years without them being confronted about sin, called into discipleship, and expected to serve others in the body, then we aren't leading well regardless of how good our sermons are. We have overestimated how much impact the sermon actually has and underestimated how important relational discipleship is in teaching people to follow Jesus.

Read Luke 14:25–33.

1. Read those last words again: "Any one of you who does not renounce all that he has cannot be my disciple" (v. 33). Think of at least one person you know who takes these words seriously. What about that person's life shows this level of commitment to Jesus? Do we expect this kind of commitment in ourselves and others, or have we become satisfied with a lesser version of Christianity?

2. What are the things in your life you care about most? Make a list. Your list could include people, possessions, status, or security. Jesus commanded us to count the cost. If He asked you to give up all the things and people on your list, would you? And if you did, would He be enough to satisfy you? Don't just gloss over these questions; stop and really ask the Lord to check your heart—and be honest about what He shows you.

The process we just went through is something the Church should take every new believer through. If it was new to you, there is a problem. Suffering is not a minor doctrine of the Christian faith; in fact, it is one of the most consistent topics in the New Testament. We can't afford to ignore it in the Church, or we risk perpetuating a cycle where we produce believers who don't know what they have signed up for.

3. What have you been taught about suffering? What do you believe about suffering? How does that compare with what the Bible says about suffering?

4. Recall from chapter 7 of *Letters to the Church* how in Iran and China people expected suffering when they became Christians. It was normal for them. When they were deciding to follow Jesus, they knew they were risking everything, including their own lives. If those were the stakes in your community, how many people in your church do you think would still profess Christianity? Would you?

It's easy to read stories about things happening overseas and feel removed from the situation, because it looks so different from what we experience here. Obviously, at least for the time being, there are going to be some differences, but have you ever considered that maybe part of the reason we don't experience as much suffering is that we aren't willing to take as bold a stand for what we believe? Our culture right now is so wary of offending anyone. It is good to be compassionate and sensitive to people's feelings, but it is never okay to do so at the price of tolerating sin or being ashamed of the gospel. We have to love people even when they don't receive it as love. Sometimes the most loving conversations are also the most awkward and potentially hurtful. We have to be willing to have hard conversations and risk experiencing rejection for it.

5. Think about times when you have shied away from having a conversation with someone for fear of how it might be received. How do you think you can overcome those fears and more willingly suffer for Jesus?

CRUCIFIED

6. How much do other people's opinions of you matter to you? How attached are you to having a good reputation and being well liked? We have to be willing to lay these things aside, when necessary, to speak the truth in love.

Have you noticed how often the Bible uses military language to describe our time here on earth? It describes a spiritual war going on constantly and calls us to be armed. Paul referred to us as soldiers, who must not get entangled in civilian affairs (2 Tim. 2:4). We've gotten things so twisted that some actually teach that life is supposed to be easier when you become a Christian. That kind of thinking is so backward and dangerous. Expectation of comfort and prosperity is a trap. It's exactly where the Enemy wants us. If we haven't counted the cost and we just expect everything to be easy, we are going to end up with a weak faith that is easily destroyed when challenges come.

7. Read 1 Peter 4:12–14. Do you expect suffering? Or are you surprised when you go through difficult times? How do you view suffering in the context of your relationship with Jesus?

Understand that the point of this is not to love suffering for the sake of suffering. We find joy in suffering because we are so enamored with Christ that we are honored to suffer for Him and with Him. We suffer willingly because we know "this light momentary affliction is preparing for us an eternal weight of glory" (2 Cor. 4:17). We suffer joyfully on behalf of other people because we love them with the love of Jesus, who loved them to the point of death on a cross.

8. Write about a time when you experienced hardship because of a decision you made out of love for Jesus or others. How did it cause you to grow? How could your attitude have been more like Jesus in the midst of the suffering?

9. Think of times when you have sacrificed something on behalf of another person. In what ways was it easy or difficult? How could you better embrace this kind of suffering in your daily life?

If someone was to punch you in the arm for thirty seconds, you would probably be extremely upset. If someone was to promise you a million dollars if you would let him or her punch you in the arm for thirty seconds, I imagine your response would be very different. You might even have a smirk on your face despite the pain, anticipating the million dollars. Nothing about your pain changed, so why such a different response? What changed? Your willingness to receive the pain changed based on your anticipation of reward for it. This is huge for the shift in our mind-set toward suffering. Jesus told us we are "blessed" when we are persecuted because our "reward is great in heaven" (Matt. 5:11–12). Jesus also said, "Sell your possessions, and give to the needy. Provide yourselves with moneybags that do not grow old, with a treasure in the heavens" (Luke 12:33). Jesus motivated our tough, sacrificial decisions with the promise that we will be glad when we're in eternity.

10. How would your decisions, big and small, look different if you made them all with only eternity in mind? What is holding you back from doing that?

11. Spend some time praying and thanking Jesus for what He suffered for you. Ask Him to give you a heart that is submissive and obedient. Ask Him to give you the courage to stand out from the world and experience rejection for Him. Ask Him to give you an eternal mind-set and a passionate love for Him and for His people.

8

UNLEASHED

*This is our heritage. This is in our DNA. We must
stop creating safe places for people to hide and
start developing fearless warriors to send out.*

VIDEO

Share session 8 from the *Letters to the Church Video Series* with your group. The video should be used at the beginning of your time together to introduce some of the concepts you will be discussing and to provide spiritual direction for the session.

DISCUSSION

Have you ever read the book of Acts and wondered where all these new leaders came from? One might think that the book of Acts would follow the remaining eleven disciples around for the entire twenty-eight chapters, but instead, you quickly see new leaders emerging and doing amazing things. Paul, Barnabas, Silas, Timothy, Stephen, and Agabus are just a few. At the beginning of Acts, no one would have guessed that Paul would be the one the narrative follows for the longest time. God clearly loves developing new leaders.

It's been said you can train an elephant, a massively powerful animal, over time to be restrained with just a string around his leg. When you take an animal and restrain it for long enough, even the strongest animals can become tame and practically powerless. When the Holy Spirit comes into people, they become a ridiculously powerful force for good in the world, but then our churches will either develop them in strength or tame them over time.

1. What is the biggest step of faith you have taken in your life? What was your relationship with God like during that season? Even if there were some aspects of it that were scary or hard, wasn't it also exciting? Isn't there a part of you that loves that feeling of total dependence on God?

If you answered yes to the last two questions, you are like the zebra in the opening analogy of chapter 8 of *Letters to the Church*. You know you were made to live by faith. This is God's desire for all His children. When we step out in faith, we get to experience more of His power, which in turn builds even greater faith and greater demonstrations of His power. We were made for this kind of a lifestyle. But it requires getting out into the wild, where things can be scary.

2. When was the last time you made a big decision—one in which your failure or success depended on God coming through miraculously? What happened? Do you make decisions like this often?

We have to fight against the temptation to remain in a state of comfort and control. If we try to control everything, we are going to miss out on experiencing the freedom and joy that come with surrendering. God wants to do powerful, amazing things through you. He wants to reveal more of Himself to you and to take you to greater depths of trust and expectancy in your relationship with Him. But it's going to require a relinquishing of control and a willingness to forego the safety of what you know.

3. No matter where you are in your walk with God, there is more of Him for you to discover. What do you tend to hold on to closely to keep you safe? Maybe it's relationships, money, a job, or living in a

certain area. There can be so many things we use to make us feel safe other than God.

4. Have you ever thought about those things being the barrier to experiencing God more? How is it that even good things can become a hindrance in our relationship with God?

5. The point is not that you have to get rid of everything but rather that you need to hold things loosely, willing to allow God to remove them whenever He wants. Are you willing to do that? What would that look like?

6. Read Ephesians 1:19–21. Do you believe that because the Holy Spirit is in you, you have access to an "immeasurable greatness" of power? How does your life reflect that?

We have conditioned people to be content with so much less than what the Bible promises we can experience. Not many of us would openly disagree with the Scriptures that tell us about the power available to us and at work in us. But often our actions and our church services tell a different story. Similarly, few of us would openly say we don't value the contribution of children to the church body, but don't our actions sometimes say otherwise? The Bible tells us we are to learn from and imitate the faith of children or we "will never enter the kingdom of heaven" (Matt. 18:3).

Could part of the issue be that we are afraid to fail? In our world today, one mistake can ruin your life. Many of us have read stories about people who posted an insensitive tweet or made one mistake on video and their lives were never the same. We have to be so careful to not make mistakes or people will pounce on us. We live in a culture that makes it difficult to be willing to step out in faith and possibly look stupid. But God has always looked for people like Jonathan who will take on a whole army with just one other guy (1 Sam. 14) or like Noah who will build a huge boat with no rain in sight (Gen. 6) or like Abraham who will set out from home with only a promise (Gen. 12) or like Josiah who will tell the whole country that they are wrong and change everything (2 Kings 22–23). These people all looked incredibly foolish, yet God moved so powerfully.

7. Have you ever stepped out in faith and regretted it? Most of us probably have no regrets as we look back on those steps of faith. Yet fear still tends to control us. How do we overcome this fear of failure?

8. What would it look like for our churches to step out in faith and see God come through in amazing ways?

There is a tendency within the Church to assume that it requires years of formal training and equipping to be able to minister effectively, but where do we find that in Scripture? Jesus' method of training was primarily opening up His life to a few people, teaching them along the way, and then throwing them into ministry opportunities and responsibility. Effective ministry does not depend on our qualifications; God has always looked for those who are full of faith, humility, and love. We need to train up believers of all backgrounds and stages in their journey to boldly and fearlessly proclaim the gospel.

9. Recall some of the amazing testimonies of the rapid multiplication of churches listed in chapter 9 of *Letters to the Church*. One example was in East Asia—a missionary saw 360 churches planted and 10,000 new believers in six months. This sort of quick spread of the gospel is happening all around the world. Do you believe God could do something similar in your city? Why or why not? What might that look like?

The early church in Acts was a powerful force. They saw and performed so many miracles, proclaimed the gospel with such fervor, and led thousands of people to Christ. But they were mostly just a group of uneducated, common people. They didn't have any kind of special training or qualifications other than spending a lot of time with Jesus. What they had was an unshakable confidence in the Spirit. As the world looked on, they knew they were witnessing a supernatural movement of God. If we start to walk with that kind of faith, we believe we will experience the same kind of power. Yet we can see that if we try to play it safe, keep things under control, not depend on God, and lean a lot on our own efforts and strategies, we won't see God work in power. Could this be why many of our churches are not experiencing God the way we see the early church experiencing God in the Bible?

10. What makes you excited about seeing God move in power in your church? What are some tangible steps you can take to help your church move in that direction? How can you be an example of faithfulness? Don't wait for structural change. Be the change.

11. Take time to pray. Repent of the times when you have doubted the Spirit's ability to work through you or any other believer. Ask God to give you fresh excitement and vision for what is possible for the Church.

9

CHURCH AGAIN

*May Your Bride become attractive, devoted, and
powerful beyond earthly explanation. May we each
become consumed with her, all for Your glory.*

VIDEO

Share session 9 from the *Letters to the Church Video Series* with your group. The video should be used at the beginning of your time together to introduce some of the concepts you will be discussing and to provide spiritual direction for the session.

DISCUSSION

As we come to our last session together, we need to be intentional with how we close it. It's so easy to care deeply about a topic while we are prompted by a book or a discussion but then let it slip from our minds once it's over. Hopefully you can see how significant the Church is to God. This isn't just an interesting topic to discuss with others. The Church is the family of God. The Church is the context through which God intends to change the world. The Church is the means through which the "manifold wisdom of God" is displayed (Eph. 3:10). We have dozens of commands in Scripture that are able to be obeyed only in the context of community (love one another, be devoted to one another in love, bear with one another, etc.).

Let's be clear on a few things.

You need to be committed to a local church, and that means way more than attending a service on Sunday. It's more like joining a family or a gang. There's a commitment not just to Jesus but to one another. This family is going to have problems. You won't agree with leadership sometimes. You will have conflict with people and maybe have some you just flat-out struggle to like. You will get offended and hurt. The temptation will be to cut and run to another body—until you find problems there, and then the cycle repeats. There's an expression that says if you find a perfect church, don't join it, because you will mess it up. Don't let the dream of a perfect family cause you to be disengaged from a good one. Though we are seeing some really amazing things here, our church in San Francisco has issues too.

At the same time, you shouldn't settle for mediocrity. We can't allow ourselves to be okay with superficial relationships, disengagement from the mission, consumer mentalities, and lack of discipleship in the church. So, the challenge is discerning what we should do.

1. How do we faithfully handle being passionate for faithfulness and possible change in the Church while also not being arrogant and divisive?

It is very important to focus on what God is asking of you, not what God might be asking of others, such as leaders in your church. When you are focused on things outside of what God has asked of you, that's often where you will end up being judgmental and divisive. Remember the example of David earlier in this guide. He was concerned with the sheep that were entrusted to him.

2. What do you think God is asking you to do to make a change, in light of all you have learned? Again, think more about repentance, caring for others, discipleship, mission, etc., than creating structural changes in your church that are beyond your control (if you aren't in leadership).

3. How will you tangibly go about making those changes? Do you need help from others? What conversations do you need to have?

Some of you are in a position of leadership over a church, where you have a say in the structure and vision of things. Some of you are thinking about planting a church in the near future. Hopefully this session was helpful for you in thinking through decisions about the structuring of the church. But all of us need to be careful that we don't get dogmatic about a model or structure and cause disunity in the body. Earlier in this study we did an exercise where we distinguished between commands from God and traditions from humans. Traditions aren't bad things. We have to make decisions on things we don't have direct commands from God on. For example, we have to decide where we are going to meet as a church, even though there is no command attached to the meeting space. We can meet in a park, house, or formal church building. There's no right answer, but we do have to wrestle with which decision best helps us obey God's commands and be faithful to Him.

That's why, while we don't all have to agree on the exact same structure, we do need to agree that structure matters. The decisions we make in our churches reflect what we value. You may want to consider whether going smaller and simpler is the right thing for you.

4. What has been your experience with smaller settings, such as community groups or small groups? How have they been helpful in ways that large gatherings aren't? How have large gatherings been helpful in ways that small gatherings aren't?

5. Often if a small group of believers are meeting in a home, people wouldn't consider it a church. Why is that? What would be your reaction to the idea of that smaller home group being an actual church? Does that feel wrong? Why or why not?

6. What is necessary for a group of believers to be a church? Think about such things as recognized spiritual leadership, a church building, paid staff, ministries, etc. What is necessary according to Scripture?

7. What would be lost by not having a large gathering with the sermon, announcements, worship band, etc.? Do you think it would be worth it if all the church's money could be used for other things? What might be some other things we could put our money toward for the mission of God?

Oftentimes one of the primary filters for making decisions in a church is what "will work," meaning what will help us get the most people there. But the filter needs to be what would please God the most. Over and over through Scripture we see God calling people to decisions that seem foolish to the pragmatic. So we must resist this temptation to see through a pragmatic lens and, instead, do whatever God wants of us.

8. Why do you think "what works" tends to drive our decision-making in the Church? How do we fight against this tendency?

Unfortunately, money plays a very large role in this drive toward "what works." Having a building and staff and a budget creates an enormous pressure to have a certain number of people. If we are honest with ourselves, most of us will admit that money affects a lot of our decisions in the Church and takes up our focus more than it should.

9. What benefits would there be to not needing money to run a church? What would be the drawbacks?

In We Are Church in San Francisco, we multiply our churches when they get to around fifteen or twenty people to keep them healthily small as well as clustered in the same neighborhood, when possible. Before you know it, we can have churches in each neighborhood of the city, intentionally reaching out to the community. Churches can spread all over without financial limitations.

10. Have you or has your church ever thought about planting churches? Which do you feel could have greater impact in a city: one church of 150 or ten churches of fifteen? Explain. There isn't necessarily a right answer, but think through practically what would be best in your city.

11. If you do feel like it would be good to raise up new leaders and plant new churches, what would be some biblical steps you could take in that direction? Close by praying for God's leading in the direction of your church.

The means through which God intends to change the world is the local church. Throughout Acts we see Paul and others boldly proclaim the gospel to those who had never heard it. Amazing conversions occurred through the power of the gospel, but that was not the goal. Paul's objective was to plant churches, not baptism centers. The goal of having a baby is not the birth but growing a family. So, as these people came to faith in Jesus, Paul began gathering with them regularly, establishing leaders, and training them how to live as family together and to reproduce what he did.

Often we have thought of the mission of God as being something distinct from the Church of God. Yet they are one and the same. The best vehicle for missions is the planting of churches, in our communities and to the ends of the earth.

Remember that there is no prescribed model of church in the Bible. There is a wide range of expressions that can be faithful to the Lord. Ultimately, it's on you and your church community to pray through the decisions that need to be made to discern what best helps us all obey God. There are resources on our website (wearechurch.com) that could help if you want to hear more about some of the choices we've made. But we want to be careful to say we should not become the authority for anyone. God and His Word are our authority. We encourage you to seek Him in His Word for direction and to continue to process through these issues within your church community and with your leaders.

"ONE ANOTHER" VERSES IN THE NEW TESTAMENT

1. "Be at peace with one another" (Mark 9:50).

2. "Wash one another's feet" (John 13:14).

3. "Love one another" (John 13:34).

4. "Have love for one another" (John 13:35).

5. "Love one another" (John 15:12).

6. "Love one another" (John 15:17).

7. "Love one another with brotherly affection" (Rom. 12:10).

8. "Outdo one another in showing honor" (Rom. 12:10).

9. "Live in harmony with one another" (Rom. 12:16).

10. "Love each other" (Rom. 13:8).

11. "Let us not pass judgment on one another" (Rom. 14:13).

12. "Welcome one another as Christ has welcomed you" (Rom. 15:7).

13. "Instruct one another" (Rom. 15:14).

14. "Greet one another with a holy kiss" (Rom. 16:16).

15. "When you come together to eat, wait for one another" (1 Cor. 11:33).

16. "Have the same care for one another" (1 Cor. 12:25).

17. "Greet one another with a holy kiss" (1 Cor. 16:20).

18. "Greet one another with a holy kiss" (2 Cor. 13:12).

19. "Through love serve one another" (Gal. 5:13).

20. "If you bite and devour one another, watch out that you are not consumed by one another" (Gal. 5:15).

21. "Let us not become conceited, provoking one another, envying one another" (Gal. 5:26).

22. "Bear one another's burdens" (Gal. 6:2).

23. "With patience, bearing with one another in love" (Eph. 4:2).

24. "Be kind to one another" (Eph. 4:32).

25. "Forgiving one another" (Eph. 4:32).

26. "Addressing one another in psalms and hymns and spiritual songs" (Eph. 5:19).

27. "Submitting to one another out of reverence for Christ" (Eph. 5:21).

28. "In humility count others more significant than yourselves" (Phil. 2:3).

29. "Do not lie to one another" (Col. 3:9).

30. "Bearing with one another" (Col. 3:13).

31. "Forgiving each other" (Col. 3:13).

32. "Teaching ... one another" (Col. 3:16).

33. "Admonishing one another" (Col. 3:16).

34. "Abound in love for one another" (1 Thess. 3:12).

35. "Love one another" (1 Thess. 4:9).

36. "Encourage one another" (1 Thess. 4:18).

37. "Encourage one another" (1 Thess. 5:11).

38. "Build one another up" (1 Thess. 5:11).

39. "Exhort one another every day" (Heb. 3:13).

40. "Stir up one another to love and good works" (Heb. 10:24).

41. "Encouraging one another" (Heb. 10:25).

42. "Do not speak evil against one another" (James 4:11).

43. "Do not grumble against one another" (James 5:9).

44. "Confess your sins to one another" (James 5:16).

45. "Pray for one another" (James 5:16).

46. "Love one another earnestly from a pure heart" (1 Pet. 1:22).

47. "Keep loving one another earnestly" (1 Pet. 4:8).

48. "Show hospitality to one another without grumbling" (1 Pet. 4:9).

49. "As each has received a gift, use it to serve one another" (1 Pet. 4:10).

50. "Clothe yourselves ... with humility toward one another" (1 Pet. 5:5).

51. "Greet one another with the kiss of love" (1 Pet. 5:14).

52. "Love one another" (1 John 3:11).

53. "Love one another" (1 John 3:23).

54. "Love one another" (1 John 4:7).

55. "Love one another" (1 John 4:11–12).

56. "Love one another" (2 John 5).

ABOUT THE AUTHOR

Francis Chan is the author of numerous bestselling books including *Crazy Love, Forgotten God, Erasing Hell, Multiply,* and *You and Me Forever*. His latest release is *Letters to the Church* (September 2018, David C Cook). His books are available worldwide and have been translated into twenty-seven languages. Chan's award-winning and innovative film series, *BASIC*, challenges Christians to reclaim the Church described in the New Testament.

In addition to founding Cornerstone Church, where he pastored for sixteen years, Francis helped launch Radius

International, which equips cross-cultural church planters with skills necessary to plant healthy, viable, and reproducing churches. He recently started Project Bayview, discipleship homes for men and women coming out of addiction or incarceration. Francis is currently a pastor of We Are Church, which is planting churches in Northern California. Francis and his wife of twenty-five years, Lisa, have seven children and one beautiful granddaughter.

WHAT IS IT THAT GOD WANTS FOR HIS CHURCH?

The *Letters to the Church Study Guide* and *Video Series* will challenge, guide, and encourage you to pursue God's magnificent and beautiful vision for His Church.

Journey with those around you—in your community, your church, or your small group—and take steps toward living out fundamental principles from the Bible. You'll see stories of transformation and hear from Pastor Francis Chan as you lean in to God's desire for the Church.

letterstothechurchbook.com

For your church.
For your small group.
For you.

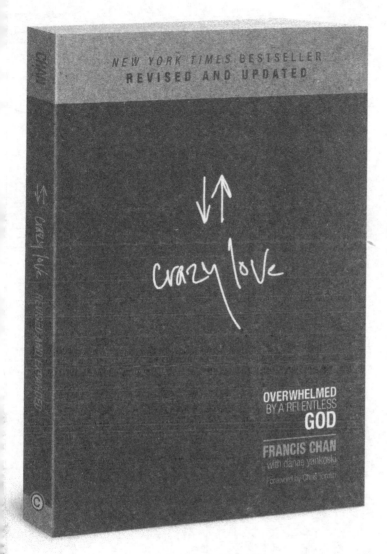

"The world needs Christians who don't tolerate the complacency of their own lives."

Francis Chan
New York Times bestselling author